Nicole L. Turner
The OYAT Group
Washington, DC

Printed in the United States of America

First Printing, 2020

ISBN 978-0-9887569-4-6
ISBN 978-0-9887569-5-3 (eBook)
Library of Congress Control Number: 2020900185

CRACKING THE ORGANIZATIONAL CLIMATE AND CULTURE CODE

Nicole L. Turner, MBA

The Culture Doctor™

Contents

Introduction 1

    What is Organizational Behavior (OB)? 1

    Why is an understanding of Organizational Behavior important to business? 3

1. Organizational Culture 5

    What do we know about Organizational Culture? 9

    Types of Organizational Culture 15

2. What Does Culture Do For Us? 16

    The Function of Organizational Culture 17

        Southwest Airlines 18

    Types of Organizational Culture 21

    Organizational Climate 25

    Culture as a Liability 30

        Barriers to Change 30

        Barriers to Diversity 31

        Culture and Money 32

3: Organizational Culture at your Company 36

    Creating and Sustaining Organizational Culture 36

    Evaluating the Type of Organizational Culture that you have 39

4. How Employees Learn Culture 42

    Stories 42

    Rituals 44

    Material Symbols 46

    Language 47

        The Case of Nordstrom: Cultural Simplicity Leads to Unrivaled Customer Service 48

Maintaining an Ethical Culture at an Organization...............50

5. Leadership 52

What Type of Leader Are You? 52

Leadership styles and the Effect on Organizational Culture and
Job Satisfaction 52

The Case of Microsoft...55

Different Types of Leaders Yield Different Cultures and
Climates 57

Transactional Leadership.......................................58

Transformational Leadership 60

Charismatic Leadership 61

Leadership Styles and Decision-Making........................63

6. Toxic Work Environments...64

How Organizations Become Toxic..................................65

Root Causes of Toxic Work Environments 68

Toxic Work Environments: The Case of Volkswagen.............72

How to Combat a Culture that is Turning Toxic 76

8. Organizational Climate and Its Effect on Employees...........79

How Employees are Affected 85

9. HR and Organizational Culture/Climate 89

Developing Organizational Culture: The Role of HR 89

HR Practices: Developing and Sustaining an Organization's
Culture 91

Bibliography 101

Appendix. Leadership Assessment 104

Appendix. Toxic Work Environments 107

Appendix. Organizational Climate...................................108

Appendix. Organizational Culture...................................109

Appendix. Maintaining a Healthy Work Environment...............110

Introduction

While the focus of this book is organizational culture and its role in shaping the workplace, we need to start by briefly describing the overarching field of *Organizational Behavior* (OB). OB scholars and practitioners are the people who study organizational culture, among other work-related psychological phenomena. They have spent years documenting workplace behaviors to give us tools to assess and address culture in the workplace.

What is Organizational Behavior (OB)?

Organizational Behavior is a field that focuses on how individuals and groups (teams) act within their working environment. The field is a unique and interesting mix of other disciplines, but relies heavily on psychology, specifically something called industrial psychology. However, OB also covers a gamut of behaviors and actions that are analyzed by borrowing a bit from different disciplines, such as sociology and economics. These scholars even incorporate neurology when they study the effects of stress on employees. Most importantly, and our focus, the study of OB can help us understand phenomena, such as organizational culture and its impact on job satisfaction and work productivity.

The climate of a work environment can easily affect job satisfaction, productivity, and your business's bottom line. OB helps us to identify behaviors, personality traits, and environments that can lead to counterproductive work environments. Some of these are intuitive, while others often fly under the radar and can cause deep divides among staff and management. Additionally, OB incorporates the tenets of psychology to help us understand the role of motivation in job satisfaction and employee behavior. The power and influence dynamic that exists among employees at different levels in the organization is also often studied, usually by analyzing leadership styles and their effect on employees. OB can also help us manage both demographic and cultural differences. Finally, OB can help us to understand tested and successful solutions to combat and prevent counterproductive work environments and deviant work behaviors.

Most importantly, the study of OB helps us to understand how we can foster positive work environments that catalyze creativity, development, and job satisfaction---elements that have been shown to reduce employee turnover and subsequently improve productivity. All in all, the discipline of OB will be our guide to ensure that we create work environments that are healthy and consequently productive.

Why is an understanding of Organizational Behavior important to business?

Organizations are made up of people. On an individual level, people have feelings, personality traits, attitudes, belief systems, perceptions, motivation, stressors, decision-making skills, communication styles, leadership styles, and different reactions to change. Now imagine putting all of the variations of these characteristics into groups and asking them to be productive. Not so easy, right? All of these differences play a role in how employees contribute to your organization.

Managers/Owners accomplish goals through people. Although many people attribute technical skills and conceptual skills to success, personal skills are just as important. Your ability to communicate, support, understand, and motivate others is critical to your success as a business leader. Therefore, improving your skills will improve your business. To

improve your skills, you have to be able to identify
and evaluate your behavior, personality traits, belief
system, perceptions, etc. Additionally, you have to be
able to identify those characteristics in your
employees.

At this point, it's imperative that I supply you
with the tools necessary to understand organizational
culture and its role in your organization. Some of this
is a bit technical but necessary. I've included some
real-world examples to illustrate the importance of
understanding organizational culture. Stick with me
through the technical stuff, and I assure you that
you'll gain valuable tools that you can use to
maintain a healthy culture that translates into
improved performance.

1. Organizational Culture

Organizational culture is "the environment in which people work and the influence it has on how they think, act, and experience work."[1] Organizational culture is the essence of a business, the 'thing' that makes the organization unique. If a business can build a strong and cohesive organizational culture, it can become a living breathing entity (think Disney and McDonalds). The success of an organization is highly dependent upon the perception of its culture. Businesses like Disney and McDonalds have become part of the fabric of American consumerism. People, especially those with children, often forget that Disney isn't just a magical land or a movie studio that produces children's cartoons. Disney is a multi-billion dollar company that has maintained its success by developing an instantly recognizable brand built on its unique culture. The organization is valued for itself, not just what it produces.

---

[1] Warrick, D. D. (2017). What leaders need to know about organizational culture. *Business Horizons*, *60*(3), 395-404.

According to researchers, there seems to be a consensus that there are seven characteristics that capture the essence of a company[2]:

1. <u>Innovation and risk-taking</u> - How many employees are encouraged to be innovative and to take risks at work.

2. <u>Attention to detail</u> - The amount of precision, analysis, and attention to detail that management expects of employees.

3. <u>Outcome orientation</u> - The degree to which management focuses on outcomes rather than the processes used to achieve those desired results.

4. <u>People orientation</u> - How much management considers the effect of outcomes on the people that work in the organization.

5. <u>Team orientation</u> - How frequently are tasks centered around working in groups or teams.

6. <u>Aggressiveness</u> - How aggressive and competitive people are that work within the organization.

---

[2] Robbins, S. P., & Judge, T. (2019). *Organizational behavior.* Harlow, England: Pearson Education Limited.

7. <u>Stability</u> - How much emphasis does management place on maintaining the status quo.

The degree and combination of these seven characteristics yield what we would call the culture of an organization. Keep in mind that culture is meant to be a descriptive term in the sense that it isn't evaluated as "like" or "dislike". Instead, it focuses on how the company is perceived, e.g., many financial businesses on Wall Street are seen as having high innovation and risk-taking, high attention to detail, high outcome orientation, low people orientation, low team orientation, high aggressiveness, and low stability. Why? Because those businesses are *perceived* as money-driven "at all costs" with minimal regard for employees. The objective of these organizations is to satisfy their shareholders and make as much money as possible, right? Maybe some, or even many, of these organizations "earned" this perception, but it certainly isn't every last one of them. How does a business distinguish itself from others within its industry, especially when that business wants to avoid a negative image? By building a unique organizational culture that makes

the company stand out from its competitors, i.e.,
Google and Facebook.

As you can probably see from the seven
characteristics listed, organizational culture is mental
by nature. Although management or corporate
policies may *formally* dictate work hours, job
descriptions, chain of command, etc., the employees'
attitude and management's response to that attitude
creates behavioral norms that form the culture of the
organization. Plainly said, the reality of how people
think and the values that they hold in an organization
determine the culture of that organization. There has
to be buy-in from employees. They are the central
component of this cognitive model. If not, the culture
will not sustain itself, and there will be
fragmentation, usually manifested as deviant work
behaviors or a lack of productivity. If everyone is not
on the same page and supportive of the
organization's mission, then at best, the organization
is performing poorly. However, many organizations
die out in the face of a fragmented organizational
culture.

What do we know about Organizational Culture?

Organizational culture is a phenomenon that affects everyone in the business world. It doesn't matter if you have two employees or 20,000, the culture of your organization affects your business, your employees, and you. The more that you know about organizational culture, the better prepared you are to combat harmful or toxic cultures. Here's what researchers know about organizational culture[3]:

- Culture is formed among groups, i.e., managers, owners, and employees. Without a group, there is no culture.

- Culture is expressed through behaviors that are developed over time, leading to both formal policies and procedures and *informal* "ways of doing things."

- Once a culture is formed, it is challenging to change. People tend to hold on tightly to their

[3] Hofstede, G., Bram, N., Daval, O. D. and Geert, S. (1990) 'Measuring organizational cultures: a qualitative and quantitative study across twenty cases'. Administrative Science Quarterly, 35: 286–316.

ideas and feelings; trying to change those ideas and beliefs is extremely difficult to accomplish.

• Different groups create different cultures. There are differences among the cultures of different businesses, even those within the same industry have different cultures.

• Culture is vague and difficult to catch, so it is difficult to measure. Unlike other data, such as earnings, culture is difficult to measure objectively.

• Anthropological terms such as 'myth,' 'ritual,' 'symbols' are commonly used to characterize culture because of its inherently social nature.

• Culture refers to ways of thinking, values, and ideas rather than concrete and objective parts of an organization.

What we should gain from this is that organizational culture is a collective state of mind. Organizational culture consists of beliefs and values that create a shared perspective. Although organizational culture doesn't include behaviors, it does include the ingredients that cause behaviors. When there is an overall company-wide consensus about what is and what is not acceptable, behavior reflects that collective understanding. If organizational culture is characterized by a customer-centric focus with the objective of relationship building, we see customer relations behaviors that are altruistic and authentic. Employees enjoy working with clients and consistently go above and beyond what they are expected to do. However, when a profit-centered mindset is pervasive in an organization, the behavior consistent with that mindset is prevalent.

We often consider "Wall Street" as a place where a profit-centered approach is most prevalent. Although that is true with some organizations, many of those organizations didn't start with that type of culture. Lehman Brothers is an excellent example of what happens to a company when toxicity changes organizational culture, leading to policies and behaviors that have serious financial implications.

Lehman Brothers was founded in 1850 and emphasized its relationships with customers and value creation. The objective of Lehman Brothers customer-centric approach was to build relationships with customers so that both the business and its customers could grow together. That culture persisted until the death of the last member of the founding family, Bobbie Lehman, in 1969.

New leadership found the pressures of shareholders and traders for higher profits to be greater than their loyalty to their customer base. A new compensation scheme was introduced that was a reflection of the shift in the organization's culture from a customer-centric model to that of a profit-oriented model. The new compensation system directly linked profits and growth to bonuses. Salary-based pay was decreased, and the bonus system pushed employees to value profits over customers. Greed became a persistent ideal of both employees and managers, ultimately serving as the impetus for deviant work behaviors.

As growth and profitability became the cornerstone of the value-system at Lehman Brothers, customers were considered secondary, the means to the desired end. Investment bankers and traders began to take unnecessary risks that were supported by the organization's culture. The culture became so pervasively toxic that managers and employees were rewarded for behaviors that would be considered unethical and even immoral by anyone's standards.

Despite indications from the global financial markets that their risky model of growth would soon be unsustainable, the directors continued to make hefty investments into risky ventures. Ultimately, the economic crisis of 2008 began with the crushing demise of Lehman Brothers. When investors went to collect their hard earn money, they were met with a resounding, "We can't pay you." Both people and entire businesses lost money, exacerbating unemployment throughout the financial sector.

What happened next is very interesting. CEO Richard Fuld was, in effect, thrown under the bus and blamed for the decision-making, but I would argue that Lehman Brothers hired the CEO that reflected the toxic culture of the business. Fuld was not the prime reason why Lehman Brothers failed; a toxic organizational culture led to the downfall of Lehman Brothers and several other businesses in the 2008 economic crisis. Richard Fuld was blamed for the failure of Lehman Brothers and subsequently punished. However, the vast majority of the employees that valued the same profit and growth "at all costs" model were not punished. Why? Because as a society, we need someone to blame. If we have someone to blame and can punish that person, then we feel vindicated. However, Richard Fuld would never have been the CEO of Lehman Brothers if he didn't fit perfectly into their organizational culture. As I stated earlier, organizational culture is hard to put your finger on, so we choose to place blame on something tangible, the CEO.

The objective of including the story of Lehman Brothers is to illustrate the direct link between organizational culture and corporate sustainability. Additionally, the objective is to highlight the fact that many of the world's businesses ignore the ramifications of a toxic work environment. Those that choose to ignore the *real* threat that a toxic organizational culture has on companies are putting their business at risk. Think about how long it took a toxic culture to develop at Lehman Brothers, mostly due to its size. How long do you think it would take a small or medium-sized business to develop a toxic work environment? This story should serve as a cautionary tale to businesses, such as small and medium businesses, that are much more vulnerable to shifts in profit. Pay attention to the culture of your organization, or you may suffer a similar fate.

Types of Organizational Culture

Organizational culture can be differentiated by whether or not the culture is deemed *strong* or *weak*. In a company with a strong organizational culture, there is a high level of agreement and commitment among employees and the perceived values of the organization. However, a company with a weak organizational culture exhibits a low level of agreement and commitment among employees and the observed values of the organization. So, which of the two is better? Well, that depends on what type of culture you are trying to build at your company or the type of culture that you already have.

If your organization is customer and employee-centric, then to build a healthy organizational culture, you'll need a strong commitment to culture. However, a strong commitment to a toxic work culture will result in an entrenched toxic work environment that will be difficult to change. The opposite is true of weak organizational cultures. If you have a weak commitment to the perceived values of the business, you won't be able to build a sustainable and healthy work environment that leads to enhanced productivity and profitability. Usually, organizations with toxic work environments will fail at some point, but those with strong cultures may take longer to do so, and the results are more catastrophic. Those organizations with toxic work environments and weak cultures can be more easily changed because there isn't a great deal of buy-in from employees. So how do you gain buy-in from your employees? Since organizational culture is linked to history, rituals, language, etc., you'll need to incorporate those elements into day-to-day operations. In a later section, we will discuss these elements in-depth, and I'll give you some tips that you can easily incorporate into daily operations that have researched and proven results for businesses.

2. What Does Culture Do For Us?

Now that you have the technical skills necessary to continue this journey, we are going to shift our focus a bit to the role of culture in organizations. Next, we will introduce a related concept called organizational climate. Then, we are going to examine the ways that culture can be a liability. Finally, an all-important section on organizational culture and money. Organizational culture does translate into dollars, so we'll pay particular attention to both the 'how' and 'why'

organizational culture translates into money—both
losses and gains.

The Function of Organizational Culture

The first important characteristic of
organizational culture, as mentioned earlier, is that it
creates a unique boundary between one organization
and the other. Second, organizational culture creates
a sense of identity for you and your employees. Next,
organizational culture creates a commitment to
something more substantial than any individual
employee. Culture sets guidelines for what is and
what is not acceptable behavior at your
organization—specifically social behavior. Finally,
organizational culture guides and shapes the attitude
and subsequent behavior of your employees.

We briefly touched upon organizational identity
or the 'essence' of an organization—the uniqueness
that makes one organization different than another.
Organizational identity is something that endures and
is a central component of how others perceive the
organization. A company's identity is tied directly to
its history, and companies go to great lengths to
maintain their identity despite external forces.
Businesses with strong organizational identity are

easy to spot. For instance, companies like Facebook, Google, Airbnb, Southwest Airlines, McDonald's, Subway, and Twitter all have strong organizational identities. You can quickly identify their logos, and their employees are the embodiment of the company.

Southwest Airlines

In 43 years, Southwest Airlines has not laid off a single employee, nor has it cut pay. Furthermore, year after year, the company pays out a yearly dividend bonus to employees that own approximately 10% of the company. How does Southwest do it?

Southwest Airlines flight attendants are known to sing, dance, make jokes, and be playful with passengers. You aren't going to receive the same type of service on any other airline. You know that you're not going to get a four-course dinner on bone china on Southwest Airlines. However, you do know that you will most likely pay far less for your airfare than you would have spent on other airlines. That's why they are successful. The company is unique and easily recognizable. Southwest's organizational identity conveys that message to you. The company has stayed true to its history and consistently outperforms other airlines with more planes and more money.

Southwest Airlines has a people-centered identity that is not only reserved for its customers. Employees are treated with the same respect that they are expected to show passengers. Southwest's mission communicates its dedication to both its customers and employees clearly and with passion:

The Mission of Southwest Airlines

The mission of Southwest Airlines is a dedication to the highest quality of Customer Service delivered with a sense of warmth, friendliness, individual pride, and Company Spirit.

To Our Employees

We are committed to providing our Employees a stable work environment with equal opportunity for learning and personal growth. Creativity and innovation are encouraged for improving the effectiveness of Southwest Airlines. Above all, Employees will be provided the same concern, respect, and caring attitude within the organization that they are expected to share externally with every Southwest Customer.

("About Southwest", 2019)

It's evident from Southwest's mission statement that they care about their employees in the same way that they care about their customers. The most important aspect of this mission statement is that Southwest *follows through* with this commitment. Therefore, the company is perceived as both credible and legitimate by stakeholders, specifically employees and customers, which breeds further success.

Your mission statement and vision are essential and drive your culture. A **Mission Statement** defines "the company's business, its objectives, and its approach to reach those objectives." A **Vision Statement** describes "the desired future position of the company." [4]Often pieces of the mission statement and the vision statement are combined to create one statement that explicates the company's purposes, its goals, **and its values**. Values is highlighted because it is so often a missing element and it simply cannot be because it describes what you *stand for*. Corporate values shape the culture and define the character of the company. These values influence the values of your employees. Later, this is described more in the

---

[4] Robbins, S. P., & Judge, T. (2019). *Organizational behavior*. Harlow, England: Pearson Education Limited.

section about how employees learn culture and values are a vital component.

Types of Organizational Culture

This section discusses the four main types of culture that researchers have discovered after decades of research on this topic: (1) Clan, (2) Adhocracy, (3) Hierarchy, and (4) Market.

Clan culture is an organizational culture that is chock full of shared values, common goals, a sense of collectivity, and a place where helping one another is part of the fabric of the company. There is a very strong emphasis on empowerment and involvement. Leaders are seen as mentors, and teamwork is the core strategy for attacking tasks. This type of organizational culture is one in which there is a strong sense of "family". The focus of the organization is collective growth. Loyalty, 'togetherness' or cohesiveness, and participation are all highly desirable qualities for success in this type of business. Southwest Airlines would be a great example of a business that has a *clan* culture.

The *adhocracy* culture is temporary, in that, it comes together quickly when presented with organizational tasks but then dismantles quickly as well. As tasks emerge, the *adhocracy* culture will come together in some form, hence the unique name *ad-hoc – "racy"*. *Adhocracy* is a culture that gives individuals a way to develop in their way, as long as they are consistent with the goals of the organization. The goal of the organization is to obtain and benefit from as many opportunities in the external environment as possible. Leaders are seen as entrepreneurs that are inspirational and who are driven by innovation. Employees will be successful if they can develop new ideas or innovate existing ones. Facebook would be a relevant example of a business that has an *adhocracy* culture.

Market culture focuses on transactions that occur in the external environment, i.e., phenomena that occur outside of the organization, instead of those that occur within the organization. The goal of this type of organization is to earn profits through competitive market interactions; earning profits is a key goal. Therefore, *market* culture stresses effective goal achieving. Competition is common among employees, which can cause limited flexibility in personal relationships. Individual achievement is paramount in this type of environment. These achievements are generally activities that connect the organization to its stakeholders. This type of culture is a "get down to business" and "get things accomplished" kind of culture. Both Amazon and Apple are good examples of businesses with *market* culture.

The fourth type of culture is the *hierarchy* culture. This type of company has a clear organizational structure, standardized policies and procedures, and very well-defined responsibilities. Mistakes are kept to a minimum because tried and true rules and guidelines are followed to the letter. The prime goal of this type of organization is stability. To achieve success in this type of organization, employees need to complete tasks with precision and follow set guidelines. Although this environment sounds restrictive, it is necessary for some industries. Organizations that operate under the auspice of the government, health care, and aviation businesses are examples of organizations that prosper with a *hierarchy* culture.

The culture within any organization can be characterized by one of the types previously mentioned. Although cultures do change (we'll look at that a bit later), in general, they are pretty stable. None of the four types of organizational cultures listed is better than the other, in general. The key is to cultivate a culture that works well, given the industry and the workplace environment. Different culture types are more successful in different industries. For instance, you wouldn't necessarily want an *adhocracy* culture at the Federal Aviation Administration (FAA) because safety is the focus. Although innovation is essential, safety is the most critical task that employees perform. Gaining an opportunity in the market is far fewer actions to administrators in the FAA than passenger safety. Therefore, a *hierarchy* culture works well in that industry. That's not to say that only one type of culture works well in a given industry. However, you will see that some companies in specialized industries perform better with certain culture types. More importantly, organizations can have more than one culture.

Sub-cultures often form in different departments within the same organization. A *sub-culture* isn't the dominant culture of the organization as a whole, but it is prevalent enough to influence the overall productivity of the organization. However, that doesn't mean that *sub-cultures* are a bad thing. For instance, if you a fashion designer and own a boutique where you sell your clothes, then you'd want salespeople that loved your brand and were motivated to sell it. You may want to develop a *clan* culture of loyalty and 'closeness' that would translate from your employees to your customers. However, the manufacturing department may be more productive if a *hierarchy* culture develops within that specific unit. Manufacturing clothing isn't an easy job and requires several steps that must be completed over and over again. Therefore, an understanding and adherence to specified policies would most likely be more beneficial to productivity. Do you see the distinction?

What type of organizational culture do you have? In the next section of this book, I will give you the diagnostic tools to evaluate the kind of culture that you have at your organization. For now, let's take a quick look at organizational climate.

Organizational Climate

Organizational culture is a critical component of organizational climate. Organizational climate refers to the shared perception that organizational members have about their company. Think *team spirit* if the two terms appear to be similar to you.

Without a culture, you can't have a climate. To create a healthy organizational climate, your employees have to have the same overall feeling about what's important to them and the company. If those two things are the same, then the employee will maintain a productive attitude and be self-motivated. Recently, researchers completed a large-scale study on organizational climate and levels of job satisfaction. They found that 4 out of 5 employees felt that a positive overall workplace led to higher levels of job satisfaction, involvement, commitment, motivation, and productivity.

These are the key features of organizational climate:

- It is the perception that employees hold about their work environment
- It is often referred to as the "psychological atmosphere"
- It gives us a quick 'picture' of the relationship between the organization and its employee
- Properties of organizational climate can be measured using appropriate instruments (you'll be given more detailed

information in the HR section of this
book)

- It is directly related to the support that
  employees feel they receive from their
  organization
- Organizational structure strongly
  influences organizational climate
- Organizational climate is a direct
  reflection of the degree of employee
  motivation
- It has both positive and negative effects
  on people's behavior in the workplace

Organizational climate can be measured, unlike
organizational culture. This fact is significant because
levels of satisfaction affect attitudes, which affect
workplace productivity. Furthermore, if you know
the type of climate that is affecting your workforce,
then you can make changes to foster a healthier
organizational climate.

Although the HR section of this book will go into
far more detail about organizational climate, how to
measure it, evaluate it, and change it, it would be
good for you and/or your employees to contemplate
the following questions:

1. Do you always receive the information that is
   needed to do your job?
2. Do you believe that you will have career
   growth opportunities in this company?
3. Are you encouraged to contribute to the
   improvement of work processes?
4. Are you always learning new things in your
   job?
5. Does clarification and guidance from your
   superiors regarding your tasks help to carry
   out your work?
6. Do your superiors help you to figure out how
   to learn and train?
7. Does the company provide training
   opportunities for everyone?
8. Do you have a career outlook that motivates
   you to work for this company?
9. Does the organization's environment facilitate
   the relationship between employees?
10. Are your colleagues always willing to help
    each other?
11. Do you trust your co-workers?
12. Do the employees of this company have a
    good relationship with each other?

13. Do other employees come to your aid when
you need their help?

14. In general, do your colleagues share
knowledge?

15. Are all employees involved in decision
making?

16. Do you believe that the time you use in your
workday is sufficient to fulfill your duties and
obligations?

17. Do you wish you had more senior
responsibilities?

18. Are you happy in your work?

19. Do you consider that your work is important
for the company to reach its goals?

20. Do you feel that working in this company
contributes to improving your life?

21. Do you believe that your work in the
company provides you and your family with
security?

22. Are you proud of this company? Do you have
friends and relatives working here?

23. When you have finished your day and go
home, do you feel fulfilled professionally?

24. Do you know the objectives of this company?

25. Do you believe that the products and services offered to the market by this company are important to society? (Veyrat, 2017)

Answers to the questions above, developed by researchers, can tell you a great deal about the climate at your organization. Do your employees feel heard? Are they proud of the company? Are they content within their current position?

Culture as a Liability

Culture can greatly enhance commitment to an organization as well as increase the consistency of employee behavior. It is a valuable tool, but we can't ignore the dysfunctional aspects of culture and their effect on the effectiveness of an organization.

Barriers to Change

Culture becomes a liability when shared values don't agree with those that will further the company's effectiveness. Often, this occurs when an organization's environment is undergoing rapid change, and the culture that is entrenched within the company is no longer appropriate. One of the many positive aspects of an effective and *entrenched* organizational culture is the consistency of behavior. For most businesses, consistent behavior is something that the organization desires for stability. However, when that behavior becomes rigid or inflexible, then the organization will suffer during times of change. There is an entire section of this book dedicated to organizational change because it is such a complex yet common issue to address. Suffice it to say, barriers to change cause businesses to collapse under the pressure of change.

Barriers to Diversity

Hiring new employees that differ from the majority of your employees in race, age, gender, disability, or other defining characteristics creates a strange paradox in companies with strong organizational cultures. Management will often want to diversify the workforce, which has shown to increase productivity significantly. However, in an organization with an inflexible organizational culture, those desired differences can slowly dissipate. When new employees join an organization with a strong and inflexible culture, they begin to assimilate and lose some of the benefits of their individuality.

These difficulties with strong cultures can cause systemic problems, so implementing appropriate strategies during the hiring and training process is crucial. That will be covered in more depth in the HR section of this book. For now, understand that there are many positive benefits to a strong organizational culture, but there are also pitfalls.

Culture and Money

A company must have a strong culture to sustain successful performance. Companies with weak cultures, as described earlier, suffer from inefficiencies in both communications and operations. If a company's employees don't subscribe to the mission and vision of the organization and don't feel a sense of loyalty, then they are unlikely to be motivated employees. Instead, these employees see their job as just…. a job. Those types of employees are easy to recognize. Apathetic employees will never yield sustained levels of high productivity because their hearts are not in it. Is that the employee's fault, or is it the company's fault? The answer can easily be both. We are going to focus on the role of the company in this section, but later we will look at the role of the employees.

Although most successful businesses are known for the amount of revenue they generate, I would argue that they should be recognized for the culture that led to this financial success. Creating that type of culture and sustaining it led to high levels of productivity. All businesses with highly successful cultures that lead to superior financial performance **must** have these three characteristics:

- The culture must be valuable—the culture has to enable organizations to behave in ways that lead to outcomes that enhance financial value, i.e., high sales, low costs, high margins, etc.
- The culture must be rare—the culture must have attributes and characteristics that are not common to all companies
- The culture cannot be easily imitated

If you take time and think about these three characteristics, they may seem intuitive. However, these characteristics are not easily attainable. If they were, then everyone would have them, and there would be no reason to discuss organizational culture.

A valuable culture is one that pushes both employees and management to perform better, faster, quicker, and with more precision. The culture, regardless of its type, should encourage that behavior and should reward that behavior. A culture that is distinguished by value-driven behaviors is one in which there is very little room for slack. That doesn't mean that employees should be followed around with a whip! It means that things like job duties, training, mission statements, customer interactions, company action, etc. are all meaningful.

For a company to meet the second characteristic, it must possess a culture that is rare. That isn't as easy as purposely doing things the opposite way of everyone in your industry. Remember, the actions also have to be valuable. Think of Southwest Airlines again. Their culture isn't rare just because they sell low-price airline fares. It is unique because they treat their employees just like their customers with everything that they do. That is rare in any industry, and it forms the cornerstone of Southwest's success.

Finally, not being easily imitated can be a bit difficult to understand. Basically, not being easily imitated means that if someone tried to imitate your culture, they would have a difficult time because it's so **unique** to who you are as people. You cannot simply take a thriving culture from another company, apply it to your company, and BAM! You are financially successful. You have to choose something unique about you and your employees and create a culture that reflects that uniqueness.

On average, every time an employee leaves, it takes 6-9 months to find a replacement. The direct costs of 6-9 months of a loss add up to a percentage of what that employee used to make, but in HR costs. For instance, if an employee earned $40,000, it'll cost about $20,000-30,000 of hiring and training costs, as well as on-the-job learning, to replace that person. The higher the level that the employee worked at, the more expensive it becomes. Furthermore, that number does not include the overall loss in productivity, which is the difference between the speed and efficiency that your last employee worked at (given they were acquainted with the organization) and the speed and efficiency of the new employee. That's a great deal of money.

Next, we are going to look at a way to identify the current culture at your company.

3: Organizational Culture at your Company

Creating and Sustaining Organizational Culture

Creating a healthy organizational culture starts with the business founders. Early on, it is far easier to create a culture that permeates throughout the organization because there are few employees. The vision of the founder becomes the culture of the organization. The owner/founder has more direct control of day-to-day activities and the overall operations of the company. Therefore, it is much easier to have direct interactions with the staff and redirect any language, actions, or routines that deviate from the norms set by the founders.

Although this sounds easy enough, founders and owners need to be particularly vigilant when setting the tones of the culture because, as I've mentioned earlier, culture endures. Therefore, the reasons why the founder created the organization will endure. If the founder finds hypercompetitive environments to be the most productive or efficient way to compete in their industry, then that culture will persist even if the environment within the industry changes. Changing organizational culture is far more complicated than creating or sustaining it because human beings are naturally averse to change, especially rapid change. Those employees that are accustomed to the *adhocracy* culture and *market* culture are usually a bit more flexible. Still, *clan* and *hierarchy* cultures are more reticent to change, which can often hinder productivity. We will examine change later in this book. For now, let's continue our discussion of creating organizational culture.

Creation of culture predominantly comes in three forms: (1) the business owner or organization leadership utilizes an HR process that hires and maintains only employees that think and feel the same way we do (2) They socialize their new employees into their way of thinking and feeling (3) The behavior of the owners or leadership encourages employees to both identify with them and to absorb their core beliefs, values and assumptions. Company successes will solidify the employees' behavior, but failures will slowly fragment the organizational culture, as company outcomes will logically challenge employees' belief systems.

This indoctrination is evident in many successful companies, such as Microsoft. CEO Bill Gates. Gates cultivated a culture of resilience and a "learn-it-all" mentality, in which employees were expected to cross-train in different departments. To this day, employee cross-training and stress management courses are a required part of the Microsoft training regimen.

Sustaining an organizational culture requires a great deal of effort on the part of the company as well. The organization maintains the organization's culture by giving employees similar experiences. These experiences are shaped during the selection process, performance evaluation criteria, training, development, and any promotion procedures. These processes ensure that those hired are a good fit with the culture of the organization, reward those employees that support it, and penalize those that don't.

It takes a bit of time and honesty to determine which type of organizational culture exists at your company, but it is well worth it. Armed with the knowledge that you have, you can implement processes to solidify or codify that culture, or you can make changes very early on in the lifecycle of the company to stop a toxic culture from forming. Unfortunately, once a culture exists, it will endure, and it is challenging to change, but it is possible. We will discuss that at length in the section on changing toxic work environments.

Evaluating the Type of Organizational Culture that you have

1. Why do you like working here, and what motivates you to come to work every day?
2. How do people at the company unwind and recharge after working hard?
3. How does the organization promote the professional growth and development of its employees?
4. How are employees here recognized for their results?
5. How does the company address failure? And success?

6. Is there much collaboration within teams and across different ones?

7. How do managers and employees share feedback?

8. Is there much room for working independently or autonomously?

9. What are the most common causes of conflict in the organization, and how is it resolved?

10. How does the company celebrate successes and achievements?

11. What activities does the company offer to promote team building?

12. What measures does the company take to give back to their local communities and those in need?

13. What are some things the company has done to

accommodate employees
with families?

14. What kind of people seem to
be the most successful here?

15. How does the organization
promote work-life balance
for its employees?

(Kununu, 2019)

These questions, adapted from Kununu's *Culture Test,* are a non-invasive way to determine what type of organizational culture is prevalent at your company. Is the organization team or process-oriented? Do employees have strong enough relationships that they are aware of other employees' after work pastimes? Are you celebrating successes frequently enough that employees take notice? Do your employees see you as charitable?

To make this questionnaire easier and anonymous, I recommend creating a digital survey using a tool like www.surveymonkey.com.

4. How Employees Learn Culture

The first step in creating an organizational culture that works for your organization is to understand what delivery methods work the best when you are trying to engrain that culture. Employees learn through the use of four fundamental delivery mechanisms: (1) stories (2) rituals (3) material symbols (4) language. These four methods have been tested numerous times by researchers and they have been shown time and time again to create a culture in the most efficient and long-lasting way. Let's take a look at these methods one at a time. Remember to think about your organization while you read through this section. What would these methods look like in your organization?

Stories

The United States is full of entrepreneurs who managed to develop novel products, which made them famous and wealthy. People like Henry Ford, Sam Walton, Bill Gates, Mark Zuckerberg, etc. all had their trials and tribulations while bringing the vision of their products to fruition. Many people know that Mark Zuckerberg dropped out of school at Harvard with no job, no degree, and a big dream.

Zuckerberg didn't believe in traditional methods of doing business, often choosing jeans and a t-shirt over an expensive suit. This *story* is part of Facebook's culture, and even today, Facebook's dress code is casual. You can bring your dog to work at Facebook, work from home, and also order a pizza if you want. The point is that the organizational culture and success of Facebook is built on Mark Zuckerberg's *story*. New employees hear this story, while executives perpetuate this story throughout the organization.

Storytelling is an effective means to create and sustain an organization's culture because it's exciting and relatable to some degree. Furthermore, *stories* form a bridge between the company's past and its present. Research indicates that employees' attitudes about their company's future improves when they can see the link between their organization's history and its present. Therefore, *stories* lead to productivity, employee satisfaction, employee retention, and improved sales revenue.

Rituals

Rituals are vital to the success of any organization and help create a culture that perpetuates the key values of any organization. These rituals can range from a daily pep talk style meeting where employees can discuss their concerns, and the group can celebrate successes while connecting those successes to the key values that the organization holds. For instance, Sam Walton began a tradition where supervisors meet daily with their employees to have a shift meeting. During this meeting, employees discuss their goals for the day, keeping in mind the values of the organization. The supervisor will then set forth an agenda that describes something 'special' that each team member is expected to do. All of these 'special' assignments are reflections of the key values that the organization holds, e.g., smile at every customer and thank them for shopping at Wal-Mart. At the end of the meeting, all employees chant "Gimme a W…gimme an A…gimme an L…gimme a squiggle…gimme an M, A, R, T!". The objective of the chant is to unite and empower employees, which is one of the key values that Wal-Mart holds. The company strives to remind employees every day that they are an important stakeholder in the organization and aren't simply expendable 'workers.' The chant was started by Sam Walton when Wal-Mart was founded in 1962. Day in and day out, Wal-Mart employees chant and positively begin their day.

Now, that's not to say that chanting is something that you have to do for your employees, but it highlights the need for a *ritual* that reminds employees of the key values of the organization. Maybe your business holds empowerment as a key-value to the success of the business. Celebrating your employees' accomplishments, birthdays, graduations, marriages, etc., will innately bond your employees to that fundamental value. Anyone can say that they value empowerment, but that becomes a 'saying' after a while. Employees focus on your actions. Those actions influence their actions. If you *show* them that you are committed to that key-value, they are much more likely to engage in behavior that manifests that key value. It truly boils down to 'mean what you say and do what you say". You have to also lead by example. Those empowerment meetings need to happen daily. If the meetings look like they are not relevant to you, then they won't be important to your employees either.

Material Symbols

Material symbols come in many forms. Their objective is to convey to employees who is important, the degree of equality that top management desires, and the appropriate kinds of behavior at the company. Those behaviors include risk-taking, conservative, authoritarian, participative, individualistic, or social, etc. The symbols that you display to your employees influence the way that they see the environment and culture of the company. If your executives fly first class and are chauffeured in limousines, and your employees take a company car, then they are very aware of the hierarchy that exists in the company. If your CEO drives a company car, the same company car that they do, then they see that being humble and conservative is an integral part of the company's value system.

Employees respond to symbols as much as they do to your actions. If you show them that all employees are equal, then they truly 'feel' the equality that is part of your value system. That isn't to say that you shouldn't reward management. Managers that drive productivity should be rewarded, but so should employees that work on 'the front lines' of your company. Maybe rewards or bonuses are or should be different between the groups, that's fine, but don't make them SO different or SO visible that employees genuinely feel subordinate to their supervisors. Your job is to *empower* your employees. If material symbols at your organization don't *empower* your employees, then you are setting up a culture that is not conducive to maximum productivity or employee satisfaction.

Language

Language acts as a common denominator to unite and engage employees, basically a common denominator among all employees. Most often, this language is unique to the organization and is used to describe equipment, management, employees, suppliers, customers, or products that relate directly to the business. At Wal-Mart, you will hear employees referred to as 'associates.' Eventbrite calls their employees 'britelings'. Pinterest calls its employees 'pinployees', while Reddit prefers 'Redditors.' These names display the individuality of the company, something that differentiates them from their competitors. It also shows uniquely united employees.

**The Case of Nordstrom: Cultural Simplicity
Leads to Unrivaled Customer Service**

Nordstrom is a Seattle-based department store that competes with the likes of Saks Fifth Avenue, Bloomingdale's, and Neiman Marcus. The company dedicates itself to customer retention and satisfaction by exceeding both industry expectations and its customers' expectations. Nordstrom associates receive discounts on clothing to 'look the part,' but most importantly, they are shown a great deal of trust by the company, which the company sees as part of its value system.

There are several incredible customer service stories, verified by Nordstrom, but I'll review just three. Nordstrom had recently moved to a new location, where the previous business was a tire store. A customer came in looking to return tires. The customer soon found out that a high-end department store had replaced his favorite tire store and was about to leave when an associate said, "Sir, Nordstrom would be happy to refund you for the tires. Let me get you the refund now." The man was stunned but grateful for the kindness that the associate showed him. The Nordstrom associate refunded the money that the man paid for the tires and wished him a pleasant day.

(1) A customer spent hours looking for the right combination of size and color for a pair of shoes that she desperately wanted to buy. Unfortunately, she was unable to locate that combination at Nordstrom. The associate contacted numerous Nordstrom stores across the country but found that only Macy's sold that color and size. The associate had Macy's ship the shoes to the woman at Nordstrom's expense.

(2) A gentleman's daughter was getting married and wanted to buy an Armani tuxedo. The Nordstrom associate informed the man that they did not have Armani tuxedos. The sales associate took his measurements just in case one was found. The next day, the customer got a phone call, informing him that the tux was available. When pressed, she revealed that using her connections, she found one in New York, had it put on a truck destined to

Chicago, and dispatched someone to meet the truck in Chicago at a rest stop.[5]

These examples illustrate to the customer that Nordstrom's associates are willing to go above and beyond the industry standards to meet their customer's needs. Nordstrom gives its employees an index card as an employee handbook. On one side of the card, it says, "We welcome you to Nordstrom, and we are so glad that you are here. Our commitment is to customer service, and we only have ONE rule". On the back of the card, it says, "Use good judgment in all situations." It is the employee's right and responsibility to interpret that. Hence, employees are empowered and inspired to excel.

Maintaining an Ethical Culture at an Organization

Managers can maintain an ethical culture at an organization by employing a few specific actions and tactics:

(1) **Be a visible role model**: Send a positive message. Employees look to the *actions* of top-level management as a benchmark for

---

[5] Robbins, S. P., & Judge, T. (2019). *Organizational behavior.* Harlow, England: Pearson Education Limited.

appropriate behavior. What you say is not as important as what you do.

(2) **Communicate ethical expectations**: Share the organizational code of ethics to employees. State the organizational code of ethics that emphasizes the values and ethical rules that employees *must* follow.

(3) **Provide training on ethics**: Develop or utilize workshops, seminars, and other training programs to reinforce the organization's standards of conduct. Top management should clarify what practices are acceptable and address any potential ethical dilemmas.

(4) **Reward ethical actions and visibly punish unethical actions**: Continuously appraise the decisions that both employees and managers make to ensure that they are consistent with the organization's code of conduct and ethics. Visibly reward those employees and managers who act ethically and conspicuously punish those that don't.

(5) **Provide formal mechanisms of protection**: Provide both formal and informal mechanisms that employees can use to report

unethical behavior without fear of retribution.
You can use ethical counselors, ombudsmen,
or ethical officers.

5. Leadership

What Type of Leader Are You?

As you move through this section, it is
essential that you evaluate yourself and compare
those results to some of the leadership styles that are
presented. Many people would like to think of
themselves as charismatic leaders, but they could be
transformational or transactional leaders or
somewhere in transition. At the end of this book, in
the appendices, you will find a self-assessment tool
that will help you to determine which type of leader
you are. I urge you to take the self-assessment, then
review this chapter.

Leadership styles and the Effect on Organizational Culture and Job Satisfaction

If you were to look up the word leadership in
a dictionary, you would probably get something like
this: "Leadership is the ability of a person to
influence a group toward the achievement of a
specific goal or set of goals." That is true, but there is
an entire dimension that a simple definition doesn't

capture. Leaders can empower and inspire; they can also impede progress and inhibit growth. As we said earlier, the owner or manager, what we would think of as the *leader*, has a responsibility to lead. He/She has the potential to create a healthy work environment (culture) or the potential to develop toxicity in the work environment that inhibits productivity. The type of *leader* that leads an organization significantly influences the organization's culture, which, as we've seen, can lead to success or ruin.

A *leader* doesn't necessarily mean the person that is formally appointed to manage the organization. Often, *leaders* arise from an existing pool of employees because of personality traits, characteristics, or experience. These *leaders* often lead in the absence of a manager that possesses characteristics of a *leader,* or they lend additional support to existing formal management. Either way, they are just as important, if not more so, than formal management.

Although overseeing day to day operations is essential, I would argue that the most critical role of a *leader* is to challenge the status quo, create visions for the future of the company, and inspire those around them to achieve those visions ethically. These tasks are not easily accomplished or easily sustained in companies. Unfortunately, some still believe that a manager's most important role, or only role, is to manage others. However, what they don't realize is that managing is a small piece of the puzzle. Finding someone with experience in management isn't as tricky a task as finding someone who can inspire and *lead* employees.

Interestingly enough, *Harvard Business Review* recently published a list of companies that were transformed by their leaders. While doing the research, the researchers discovered an interesting trend. Many of the CEOs that led the organizations to success either had no experience in that industry or worked their way up after years of service to the company. That means that the vast majority of CEOs had no executive leadership experience, i.e., no formal training. Those CEOs that had no experience brought a fresh perspective, such as Jeff Bezos of Amazon. Other CEOs were regular employees that envisioned more for the company and led their own projects, creating a vision for the future that their co-workers could follow, such as Satya Nadella of Microsoft. The employees that rose to the 'top job' of

CEO were deemed "insider outsiders" by the researchers because, although they worked within the company, they had no prior experience as executive leaders or CEOs. They were hired or promoted because of their ability to create a vision that others could follow. [6]

The Case of Microsoft

Microsoft was known for its cautious culture for decades. Software engineers took years to come up with new and improved versions of existing products. They tested every area methodically and approved every adjustment. However, when software engineer Satya Nadella became CEO, the old way of doing things wouldn't work in the dynamic software market. Therefore, Nadella knew that he had to change the culture of Microsoft from risk-averse to a culture characterized by risk-taking. Additionally, Nadella had to institute a cultural change that would transform Microsoft into a market-oriented business that was continually scanning the environment for more opportunities.

---

[6] Anthony, S., & Schwartz, E. (2017, May 8). What the Best Transformational Leaders Do. *Harvard Business Review*. Retrieved from https://hbr.org/2017/05/what-the-best-transformational-leaders-do

Nadella isn't known for engaging speeches and is quite unassuming. Some have even described him as quiet. However, Nadella took his natural predilection to analyze situations and formed his distinct leadership style characterized by listening, learning, and analyzing. Nadella spent much of his time with employees and management who understood all the facets of their respective departments and listened to their concerns and ideas. He allowed employees and managers to *teach him* about their jobs.

Nadella incorporated additional strategies to empower his employees, such as a company-wide *hackathon*, in which employees spend the day working on special projects that are employee-driven. Although the event is named the *hackathon*, coders are not the only employees that attend the event. The *hackathon* consists of Microsoft employees from all over the world that work in a variety of positions within the company who come together to share their unique projects in cross-disciplinary self-organized teams. The approach is successful because employees drive the projects, form their own teams (or choose to work on several different projects in different capacities), and these cross-disciplinary teams employ their diverse problem-solving skillsets to develop cutting edge products or services that fulfill their own unique interests, and the strategic vision of the company.

Empowerment is a powerful tool that effective leaders can utilize to engage employees and increase satisfaction and productivity by developing a healthy organizational culture. To cultivate that culture, the powers that be need to choose leaders that are *transformational* as opposed to those that are *transactional*.

Different Types of Leaders Yield Different Cultures and Climates

Different types of leaders will ultimately yield different types of organizational cultures and climates. Their effect on employees significantly influences employees' behavior that eventually affects the relationship between the company and its customers. There is a myriad of different types of leaders, so I'd like to take a bird's eye view of leadership in this section and limit the discussion to *transformational* vs. *transactional* leaders, as well as *charismatic* leaders. Then, touch upon some of the most prevalent forms of leadership styles, mostly positive, and the behaviors that those leaders exhibit.

As we have already seen, actions always speak much louder than words. A leader's behavior is the single most crucial ingredient to the creation of organizational culture and climate, so it is vital that you understand those behaviors so that you can incorporate them into your behavior.

Transactional Leadership

Transactional leadership is characterized by leaders that are task and goal-oriented that focus exclusively on leading their employees to an established outcome. These leaders maintain the goal as the driving force behind all of their decisions. Transactional leaders don't spend much time focusing on other aspects of the business, such as the mission, vision, employee satisfaction, etc. Employees know their roles and their responsibilities and understand the hierarchy of decision-making. Basically, "stay in your lane" and accomplish this, and you'll move up in the company. I'm sure that you can see how this can be problematic. Some transactional leaders employ *quid pro quo,* i.e., "you do this for me and I'll do this for you." Often, some see business operations as a transaction, hence the name *transactional. Transactional* leaders are concerned with their self-interests more than that of the company.

Although *transactional* leaders recognize excellent performance and reward that performance, they often see the relationship as a contract where certain behaviors receive certain rewards. Every reward is contingent upon performance and specific actions that lead to the ultimate goal. *Transactional* leaders manage by exception. That means that they either watch employees and look for deviations from the rules and standards, or they only intervene if standards are not met. Finally, they often abdicate responsibilities and only make decisions when they have to. Otherwise, they spend time actively avoiding decision-making.

Additionally, and most detrimental to building an ethical culture, transactional leaders often get lost in the trees and forget about the forest. They see one goal after the other and don't usually "zoom-out" to see the big picture or the greater good. Transactional leaders don't inspire or engage employees in the way that transformational leaders do, and don't create the same types of cultures that transformational leaders do.

Transformational Leadership

Transformational leaders are those leaders that put aside their self-interests for the greater good of their staff and the company. These leaders provide vision and a sense of mission. They strive to instill pride in their employees and gain their respect and trust. They communicate high expectations and purpose, but in ways that are digestible to their audience. They try and intellectually stimulate employees by promoting intelligence, rationality, and problem-solving skills. Finally, and most important to creating an ethical organizational culture, *transformational* leaders give employees personalized attention, treat their employees individually, and both coach and advise their employees. These leaders exact sustainable change in organizations and shape productive organizational cultures that promote productivity and employee satisfaction.

Transformational leaders exhibit high levels of creativity, which often deviates from established standards and norms. However, they are successful, in part, because of those deviations. The case of Microsoft illustrates that a *transformational* leader can change the organizational culture of a company and subsequently reposition the company in the market. Microsoft is a market leader, at least partly, because of the culture that its leader cultivated.

However, to be a success, leaders must possess positive attributes from both *transactional* and *transformational* leadership. A leader that gives personalized attention to employees but doesn't maintain specific goals and benchmarks may be personable, but they are often ineffective business leaders because they don't reach those goals. In contrast, a leader that is a "taskmaster", but isn't able to express the company's vision and empower employees will also be ineffective. You can look at *transactional* leadership as the "bare minimum". *Transformational* leadership **builds** on the necessary foundation of *transactional* leadership. When you have both, you have all the ingredients required to create success through the creation of a productive organizational culture led by an effective and capable leader.

Charismatic Leadership

Charismatic leaders are those leaders that are transformational, but also exude charisma and uniqueness. These leaders are often famous and include people like John F. Kennedy, Martin Luther

King Jr., Ronald Reagan, Bill Clinton, Steve Jobs, and Mary Kay Ash. Although *transformational* and *charismatic* leaders share several qualities, they are not precisely the same. *Charismatic* leaders have a vision that is expressed as an idealized goal. That goal proposes a better future than the status quo, and they can clarify the importance of that vision so others understand it. *Charismatic* leaders are willing to take high personal risks, incur high costs, and are self-sacrificing. They possess a particular sensitivity to the needs of their followers. These leaders are perceptive and can anticipate the needs of others. Finally, *charismatic* leaders engage in unconventional behaviors that people perceive as unique and memorable. *Transformational* leaders can become *charismatic* leaders, but *transactional* leaders cannot. That doesn't mean that *charismatic* leadership is better than *transformational* leadership. Both forms of leadership can be extremely effective. Keep the case of Microsoft in mind. Nadella is not known for his charisma and unique behavior, but he is an amazingly effective leader.

Charismatic leaders are incredibly persuasive, which can be problematic. Although these leaders can articulate a vision and quickly "sell it" to their followers, that vision isn't always a healthy one. *Charismatic* leaders are self-sacrificing for their idealized greater good, which means that these leaders can discard things and people that are counterproductive to the realization of their vision. Adolf Hitler is an excellent example of a *charismatic* leader whose vision was detrimental to the world, but he was able to convince his followers that it was in their best interest.

Leadership Styles and Decision-Making

Leaders employ different styles of leadership that result in different outcomes, depending upon the type of leader and the situation. There are many leadership styles, so once again, I'll create a bird's eye view and focus on three styles of leadership centered around decision-making: autocratic, democratic, and laissez-faire.

Autocratic leaders make all the decisions themselves and rarely if ever, consult their employees. They expect obedience from employees and don't leave room for dissenting opinions. Democratic leaders make the decisions themselves, but they consistently consult their employees and incorporate both supporters and dissenters into their final decision. Finally, Laissez-faire leaders shun decision-making and leave the decisions up to either the employees or members of management. They are usually not involved in the day to day operations of the company.

Don't assume that one or two of these styles is better than the other in every circumstance. For example, when a life or death decision, such as those that experienced surgeons make, needs to be made quickly, democratic leadership may not serve you well. More than likely, an autocratic leadership style would be most conducive to a positive outcome. If the owner or head of a company is a terrible and ineffective leader, then you may want that person to have a laissez-faire leadership style so that more effective people can make the decisions.

6. Toxic Work Environments

Toxic work environments develop directly out of organizations with an extremely unhealthy organizational culture that *fails* to address those issues promptly. Preventing the development of a toxic work environment is far easier and less costly than attempting to correct a culture that is already toxic. Therefore, we will begin this section discussing how you can identify the "seeds" of a toxic work environment and take immediate action to address the issues before the toxicity becomes ingrained in the culture. We will also take a look at what can be done after the culture sours and turns toxic.

How Organizations Become Toxic

Although employees may face unrealistic demands or painful emotions at work, these events aren't toxic by themselves. However, they can serve as the seeds that sprout toxicity. When people feel that their confidence, hope, pride, and/or self-esteem has been taken from them, they can become toxic. Additionally, the insensitivity of others (co-workers) or apathy toward mistreatment can serve as a seed.

Toxicity begins slowly. Often, it goes unnoticed until it is too late. People start to disconnect from their work slowly. Deadlines become an afterthought. Unlike employees that still have loyalty and commitment to the company, these employees won't exhibit signs of feeling "overwhelmed". At this point, they don't place any emphasis on deadlines or the quality of their work. The quality of their work has been poor for some time, as they begin to focus exclusively on the pain that they feel and the perceived sources of that pain---

the company usually or members of executive leadership/management. Therefore, you need to be aware of what I call the *pre-toxic* stage of organizational culture decline.

The *pre-toxic* stage of organizational culture decline is the period right before culture turns toxic. During this stage, employees will exhibit behaviors that are indicative of toxicity to come---these are the proverbial "red flags" that you need to look out for. These behaviors are pretty obvious if you are paying attention, and they are your best opportunity to take control before the organization becomes toxic, which is extremely difficult to come back from. When I say difficult, I mean that the vast majority of organizations will fail in attempting to change a toxic work environment—think of Enron, Tyco, and WorldCom. Unfortunately, the phrase "too little, too late" can be applied in this context.

During the *pre-toxic* stage of cultural decline, you should be able to see signs of stress and being overwhelmed, as well as a bitterness developing among employees. These behaviors include an increase in absenteeism, turnover, illnesses among employees (as stress causes both emotional and physical illness), lack of commitment to company goals, cliques among employees, and poor working relationships between leaders and employees.

Absenteeism can be both strategic and illness-induced. We know that stress causes illnesses because it put undue pressure on our immune system, causing it to be less effective. However, there is also something that I refer to as *strategic* absenteeism. This type of absenteeism is purposeful, and the objective is to harm the company. For instance, if one specific employee closes all deals and is the only employee that knows how to close those deals, but that employee chooses to be spiteful and is "sick" on that day. Spitefulness is a tell-tale sign of toxicity building in your organization.

I don't mean to sound fatalistic, but once a culture becomes *genuinely* toxic, the toxicity is engrained in not only the employees but also the task environment. The way that people perform their work fundamentally shifts. Changing that type of environment is challenging and takes quite a bit of change from all levels of the organization. Therefore, a commitment to change is the main ingredient of a successful shift in organizational culture.

To understand toxic work environments, we need to understand what causes them to arise, leading to our next section.

Root Causes of Toxic Work Environments

According to organizational culture researcher Peter Frost, known for his work with toxic work environments, there are seven critical sources of toxicity in the workplace: intention, incompetence, infidelity, insensitivity, intrusion, institutional forces, and inevitability.[7]

- Intention-the intentions of leadership concerning their interactions with employees create an environment that is either conducive to toxicity or isn't. Leaders can choose cooperative or democratic styles of leadership, as previously discussed, or they can choose autocratic forms of leadership—using fear as a tool. Those leaders that employ fear create a breeding ground for toxic work environments because employees are consistently undermined, and their self-esteem is attacked.

---

[7] Frost, P. J. (2004). Handling Toxic Emotions:: New Challenges for Leaders and their Organization. *Organizational Dynamics, 33*(2), 111-127.

- Incompetence-Managers are often promoted based on outcomes and their "hard" skills—technical skillset. These skills are revered much more than "soft" skills—people skills. Being a fantastic financial analyst doesn't mean that you have the skill set to manage financial analysts. Managers promoted based solely on their hard skills don't make effective leaders. They usually micromanage their employees because they don't understand the boundary between their strategic role and their daily operational role. Micromanaging leads employees to abandon creativity and their intrinsic drive to succeed. Instead, those feelings are replaced with bitterness and resentment.

- Infidelity-Betrayal of an employees' emotions or concerns is one of the worst forms of toxicity within an organization. When an employee divulges information to a manager, that information should be seen as confidential in all respects. Unfortunately, some managers see personal value in that information and utilize it to leverage relationships with others or even use it as fodder for gossip. That betrayal felt by the employee not only affects that one employee, but it also affects any employee that is a witness to the situation. The learned lesson is: "Don't ever trust our manager".

- Insensitivity-the inability of management to understand the emotions of their employees is detrimental to organizational culture. Ultimately, some managers are 'emotionally intelligent' and those that are not. Managers that do not possess emotional intelligence (the ability to 'read' the emotions of their employees) run the risk of harming their relationships with their employees. Often, these managers think that everyone can "check their feelings at the door", which is entirely unrealistic.

- Intrusion-this situation often occurs when there is a charismatic leader. As noted earlier, charismatic leaders will often persuade followers to follow their vision for the company. At the extreme, employees begin to experience an unhealthy balance between their work and personal lives. The leaders' vision for the company starts to take control of facets of their lives that are unrelated to work, and employees find themselves bringing work home with them—mostly emotionally. When something goes awry, employees are left feeling resentful that they sacrificed so much for someone else's vision and withdraw their commitment and loyalty to the organization.

- Institutional Forces-these forces are company-specific and refer exclusively to policies and procedures that the company utilizes to reach their desired outcomes. These forces are usually thought of as the formal policies, although you can certainly see the effect of institutional forces on informal 'policies' that the business follows. Institutional forces become an issue and lead to toxicity in work environments when people are reduced to numbers and processes. Once a company begins to view its employees as 'factors of production' as opposed to people with feelings, needs, and desires, then employees start to sense that and withdraw their loyalty.

- Inevitability-There are types of emotional pain that cannot be avoided at work, such as trauma, but a company with a well-developed system for dealing with emotions at work will be more likely to persevere these episodes. Those companies that do not have well-developed systems or those with maladapted systems will find themselves unable to deal with these issues effectively.

These seven critical areas serve as foundational forces in creating toxic work environments. However, they also serve as a guide to combatting toxic work environments. By identifying the seeds of toxic work environments in your company, you can take action before the culture turns completely toxic. I recommend looking to the appendices to take a few of the quizzes listed to see where you stand in terms of toxicity at your workplace.

Toxic Work Environments: The Case of Volkswagen

Martin Winterkorn was named the CEO of Volkswagen in 2007. The car industry was undergoing a vast transformation, one that many felt was putting enormous pressure on all car manufacturers. Products were being heavily influenced by cutting edge technology, and consumer tastes shifted quickly. The dynamic market meant that car manufacturers had to anticipate consumer preferences and the demands of policymakers.

Winterkorn developed an ambitious growth program, Strategy 2018, whose main goal was to propel Volkwagen ahead of General Motors and Toyota as the global leader in car manufacturing by 2018. Volkswagen was already the European leader in car manufacturing and felt that the goal of becoming the global leader was the next logical step. As part of the plan, Volkswagen took a very different path by betting on clean diesel fuel, as opposed to exploring hybrids to upgrade the traditional internal-combustion engine. "Clean" diesel was purported to increase performance and gas mileage while burning cleaner—being better for the environment.

However, the engineers hit a roadblock in 2007 when the US's Environmental Protection Agency implemented stricter emissions standards that would block Volkswagen's ability to sell their new "clean" diesel vehicles in the US. Executives knew that they needed the US market to become a global leader in car manufacturing. Most importantly, the top-down culture that developed at Volkswagen was toxic. Engineers were told that management didn't want to hear about any problems they encountered and were regularly threatened with being fired. The CEO Winterkorn and the marketing team developed an enormous and expensive US-focused marketing campaign and told engineers that they didn't care *how*, but the cars had better pass EPA emissions.

The only technical fixes that were at their disposal would take a few years before Volkswagen could develop pollution-abatement equipment sufficient to meet the EPAs diesel regulations. The engineers were desperate to keep their jobs, so they turned to another option. There was software in Europe used for emergency vehicles and construction equipment like bulldozers and cranes that permitted regulators to override pollution controls in short spurts when high engine performance was required. The engineers at Volkswagen took the concept a step further. They expanded the software's capabilities enabling it to detect when a stationary emissions test was taking place and alert the engine-control system to adjust catalytic converters and exhaust systems to reduce pollutants. That 'quick fix' made the EPA happy and pleased their overbearing and threatening boss Winterkorn. The engineers kept their jobs, and

Volkswagen sold approximately 500,000 vehicles in the United States.

However, the scam eventually made its way to the EPA and European officials. Volkswagen was caught red-handed as the software was easily detectable once regulators knew what to look for. Volkswagen was ordered to pay the largest class settlement in US history: $14.7 billion. "Volkswagen turned nearly half a million American drivers into unwitting accomplices in an unprecedented assault on our environment," said Attorney General Sally Yates. Sales of Volkswagens plummeted in the US and have slowed significantly in Europe, their most significant and most lucrative car market.

Why would engineers take this risk? For their livelihoods. Volkswagen's executive management created an unhealthy organizational culture in which fraudulent behavior was rewarded as long as it led to their desired outcomes — winning no matter what led Volkswagen down a losing path.

How to Combat a Culture that is Turning Toxic

As I stated before, you are more likely to be successful in combatting toxic work environments as early as possible, preferably during the *pre-toxic* stage. Despite the complexity of human emotions and the differences among industries, researchers have found three basic but powerful ways to change organizational culture:

1. Identify what's working and address what isn't.
2. Ask employees for feedback.
3. Write a company statement that proclaims your company culture.

I would say that inherent in these three basic steps is a desire to change and a commitment to change. If you genuinely want to change the culture at your organization, then you are willing to make substantive changes that include your relationship with the company. I would rewrite these and add a few steps to include the following:

1. Talk to your employees to identify what is and what is not working.

2. Write plans to correct the deficiencies and institute change one project at a time—make sure that employees are the driving force behind the projects.

3. Solicit employee feedback to help you determine the efficacy of the projects that you put into place.

4. Write a company statement that proclaims your company culture.

You identify what's working and what isn't through your interactions with employees. Employees are in the "know". They are your front-line soldiers and understand the inner working and processes of your company, probably better than you do. Have the humbleness to ask them what is and what is not working. Employees, like all people, want to be heard. Listening to them will give you the valuable information that you need, but most importantly, it will instill a sense of value in your employees. A sense of value is the antithesis of toxic work environments. An employee with a sense of value and belonging will maintain their loyalty and commitment to a company, which is exactly what we want in a healthy work environment.

Writing and developing plans of action is a critical step in the change process. Make sure that employees drive these projects, not only by assigning them lead roles, but also assuring that the plans are borne out of a consensus. Your approach to these plans will fundamentally shift from top-down to bottom-up, yielding fruitful avenues toward change.

Ask for brutally honest employee feedback on the projects that you initiate. Most importantly, be willing to make significant changes to these projects based on employee feedback. Check your pride at the door! Your objective is to make this company flourish not to get praise for your plans. Keep that in mind or you may find yourself without a company…plain and simple.

Once you have solidified your plans, write a full statement that proclaims your company's culture in descriptive terminology that reflects the overall sentiment of the organization. Make the statement clear and concise. Most importantly, make it meaningful. If you remember our example of Southwest Airlines, the airline supported its mission and value statements with real and visible actions. Your focus should be on sustaining the message that you create. Know this: If you fail to achieve the goals in your statement, then you will further solidify negative employee sentiments and employees will have less faith in the organization than they did before. You will most likely find yourself in a toxic environment that is now even more difficult to change.

8. Organizational Climate and Its Effect on Employees

Organizational climate is defined as the shared perceptions of and the meaning attached to the policies, practices, and procedures employees experience and the behaviors they observe getting rewarded and that are supported and expected[8]. There are six dimensions of organizational climate[9]:

1. Clarity-refers to knowing what is expected from you and understanding how those expectations directly relate to the goals set forth by the organization.

2. Standards- Emphasis that management puts on improving performance and the degree to

---

[8] Schneider, B., Ehrhart, M. G., & Macey, W. H. (2013). Organizational climate and culture. *Annual review of psychology*, *64*, 361-388.

[9] Permarupan, P. Y., Saufi, R. A., Kasim, R. S. R., & Balakrishnan, B. K. (2013). The impact of organizational climate on employee's work passion and organizational commitment. *Procedia-Social and Behavioral Sciences*, *107*(2013), 88-95.

which challenging but attainable goals are set.
Additionally, standards tell employees what
level of mediocrity is tolerated.

3. Responsibility-the feeling that you have both
   authority delegated to you and that you can do
   your job without being micromanaged. Also,
   there is a level of accountability.

4. Flexibility-the degree to which you feel there
   are no unnecessary rules or procedures within
   the organization, and the feeling that new
   ideas are easy to get accepted by others,
   including management.

5. Rewards-being recognized for good work,
   and the degree to which recognition is directly
   related to levels of performance.

6. Team commitment- feeling proud and
   expressing pride in belonging to the
   organization, as well as trusting that everyone
   works towards a common objective.
   Additionally, working positively together and
   cooperating across organizational structures.

Researchers argue that each of these dimensions
influences the amount of *passion* and *commitment*
that employees feel toward their organizations. Work

passion is defined through several different dimensions including[9]:

1. Meaningful work- Employees perceive an organization's larger purpose, consider their work to be worthwhile, feel pride for their individual contributions that help the organization serve its target market.

2. Collaboration-employees perceive an organizational environment and culture that enhances collaboration, cooperation, and a level of encouragement among all organizational members at all levels within the organization.

3. Fairness-employees perceive the work environment to be fair in terms of pay, benefits, resources, and workload. People treat each other with respect, and leaders act in an ethical manner.

4. Autonomy-employees perceive an environment where people have the tools, training, support, and the authority to make decisions.

5. Recognition-Employees perceive an environment where they are praised, recognized, and appreciated by colleagues

and their leader for their accomplishments, and where they are contributing to relationships in a positive manner.

6. Growth-employees perceive a work environment, in which, employees have opportunities to learn, grow professionally, and develop skills that lead to advancement and career growth.

7. Connectedness with the leader-employees trust their leader and leaders make an effort to form an interpersonal connection with employees.

8. Connectedness with colleagues-employees perceive an environment where they trust their colleagues and where their colleagues make an effort to form an interpersonal connection with them.

Finally, researchers define organization commitment as: "An attitude reflecting an employee's loyalty to the organization, an ongoing process of expression for the organization and its continued success and well-being"[10].

---

[10] Northcraft, G. B., Neale, M. A., Tenbrunsel, A., & Thomas, M. (1996). Benefits and burdens: Does it really matterWhat we allocate?. *Social Justice Research, 9*(1), 27-45.

In the earlier section on Organizational Climate, I introduced a survey of 25 questions that you could utilize to catalyze conversations and gain a more profound understanding of your organization. The answer to these questions will help you to determine where your organization falls along the climate spectrum.

Additionally, I think that including this quiz within the text is essential before you move on to the other material in this section. I want you to be able to create clear distinctions in your mind between ethical organizational climates and unethical organizational climates (described next).

Evaluate each of these based on the following Likert scale[11]: (1) disagree fully (2) disagree (3) slightly disagree (4) neutral (5) slightly agree (6) agree (7) agree fully.

1. Ethics goals and objectives are as important as production, quality, and financial goals and objectives.

---

[11] Dallas, L. L. (2003). A Preliminary Inquiry into the Responsibility of Corporations and Their Officers and Directors for Corporate Climate: The Psychology of Enron's Demise. *Rutgers LJ*, *35*, 1.

2. Leaders regard their ethical responsibility to be as, or more important than, any other responsibility.

3. The organizational focus is on ethical behavior, not just on ethics-related rhetoric.

4. The ethics strategy deals with key stakeholders (e.g. employees, customers, suppliers, competitors, unions).

5. Guidelines exist to assist leaders at all levels in making appropriate decisions on ethics.

6. Employees know how to obtain guidance when facing an ethics-related question for which no policy exists.

7. People believe there is a direct connection between ethics goals and objectives and their individual success.

8. Employees at all levels have ethics goals and objectives for which they are held accountable.

9. Employee adherence to ethics policies and procedures is regularly monitored.

Finally, I highly recommend educating yourself on the appreciative inquiry model, which takes these questions a step further, leading to vibrant and dynamic interactions among employees. I have included several links in the appendix to this section so that you can educate yourself on the use of the model in your organization.

How Employees are Affected

An unhealthy organizational climate manifests in several types of behaviors that fall on a spectrum. As the climate within the organization becomes more and more unhealthy, the behaviors begin to become more harmful. Unfortunately, as discussed in the previous section, once you hit *toxic*, it's challenging to return to a healthy organizational climate. I envision that spectrum to look like this:

Dangerous Behavior-physical agression, emotional abuse, sexual harassment

Illegal Behavior-theft, vandalism, sabotage

Spiteful or Vindictive Behavior-forming cliques, starting rumors that harm the company, retaliation

Resentment--anger expressed through absenteeism, excessive lateness, and witholding effort

Emotional Disconnect--apathy, late work, quality of work diminishes

As we move up the hierarchy, the colors become darker to indicate more deviant behaviors exhibited by affected employees. The hierarchy begins with a fundamental emotional disconnect, which can be addressed very early on. When you see these behaviors, intervene immediately. However, this is also a time to reflect on the climate of the organization as a whole. I'm not talking about the actions of one employee, although you should certainly address those appropriately. I'm talking about an overall general sense of emotional disconnect among staff. Are major factions in your department or unit showing a general reduction in the quality of their work? Are they apathetic to both deadlines and the impact that their work has on others?

If we fail to notice emotional disconnect or fail to act on it effectively, then we move quickly to resentment. As discussed earlier, there are two forms of absenteeism: (1) absenteeism due to illness-stress-induced and non-stress-induced (2) strategic or resentful absenteeism-the objective is to harm the company in some way. Resentment leads to resentful absenteeism. This is a mild form of sabotage, which we will see later. At this point, your organization is becoming toxic quickly. Intervening and following the steps in the previous section to "re-boot" your commitment to culture is critical to stopping the evolution of this behavior to the next level.

Spiteful or vindictive behavior is the first level of full toxicity, in my opinion. These behaviors occur when formal and informal policies no longer hold meaning to the employee. Both employees and management become victims and aggressors in this type of environment. Employees begin to form cliques and bully one another, as well as bully management. Management forms cliques and start to suffer from something called "group think"—this occurs when members of management think in the same way and exclude anyone that disagrees with them.

Illegal behavior is self-explanatory. When I say stealing, I don't mean stealing time by being late. I am referring to the unlawful act of theft, which may include property or a company's proprietary information/processes. At this stage, your organization is in freefall and the culture is pervasively toxic.

Finally, dangerous behaviors refer to behaviors that are void of any formal or informal sense of self, others, or dignity. These behaviors, although rare, do occur at organizations. At this point, I highly recommend getting law enforcement involved. Most logical adults would have intervened at this point. However, not always. If you allow your organization's employees and climate/culture to reach this level—there isn't anything in this book that is going to help you solve the issue.

The moral to the story is---intervene! Don't sit idly by and watch these behaviors escalate because they will. If you are an employee and you are witnessing these types of behaviors, then immediately speak to someone. If that person won't listen, try to speak to someone else. If you know that your concerns are going to fall on deaf ears, then plan on leaving the organization. These types of behaviors and this atmosphere will begin to affect you both mentally and physically.

9. HR and Organizational Culture/Climate

I would argue that the role of HR is most critical to creating, maintaining, and changing organizational culture and climate. From the onboarding process to annual reviews and exit interviews, HR sets the tone for the organization from the very beginning of an employee's experience.

Developing Organizational Culture: The Role of HR

Although we have spent a great deal of time defining organizational culture and climate, as well as how to maintain and change a culture, this section is explicitly dedicated to the role of HR. HR is one of the most influential departments in any company. HR is responsible for ensuring that strategy is not only limited to business goals but also an organization's most valuable asset—it's people. To help foster a healthy organizational culture, members of the HR team should aim to do the following:

- Be a role model for the organization's beliefs- this can be most effectively accomplished through actions more than words.

- Reinforce organizational values-HR can accomplish this by developing processes that are driven through the values of the organization.

- Ensure that organizational ethics are defined, understood, and practiced by all members of the organization.

- Enable communication and feedback channels among organizational members.

- Define employees' and management's roles, responsibilities, and accountabilities.

- Provide continuous learning and training.

- Develop and sustain the reward and recognition processes.

- Encourage team-building and individual empowerment.

- Recognize and solve both individual and organizational problems and issues while employing the organization's values.

HR Practices: Developing and Sustaining an Organization's Culture

HR has several essential functions during the development of an organization's culture. These include hiring practices, onboarding efforts, recognition programs, and performance management programs.

- Hiring Practices: The main goal of HR should be to assess organizational fit throughout the hiring process. Some of these include the following:
  - Interview questions should focus on areas that complement the organization's vision, mission, and value statements. For instance, if the organization is in a technologically advanced and dynamic industry, then applicants should possess a natural curiosity for how things work.
  - Interview questions should contain questions that elicit comments about the organization's values, such as a commitment to customers. If the candidate focuses intently on bad experiences with customers, then

perhaps the applicant doesn't fit into the organization's culture and should not be hired.

- o It is vital that you do not discuss the company's culture upfront. In fact, don't tell the candidate anything about the culture of the organization if that's possible. Instead, listen to their experiences and their beliefs to determine whether or not they fit within the organization.
- o Make sure that you are giving the applicant an accurate picture of the organization, not what the organization would like to become. Unfortunately, giving the candidate the truth upfront will save you from additional turnover or an unhealthy organizational culture.

Despite the natural inclination to 'talk up' your organization, be careful. Turnover costs are between 50% and 150% of the salary of the position that needs to be filled and the costs continue to climb. Unfortunately, it doesn't pay to be dishonest with candidates. They have very little loyalty to the company, as they are new, and they have no problem leaving a new job---we have lots of statistics that show that trend. Therefore, be your BEST you, but also represent an honest version of your company.

According to SHRM (The Society for Human Resource Management), there are five interview questions that every recruiter should ask candidates[12]:

1. What are three negative personal qualities that someone close to you would say that you possess?

    a. Why three, right? Well, it seems that anyone can come up with one of these answers, even two. However, coming up with three of these answers pushes you both intellectually and psychologically. People that are good at interviews always have a backup answer, which they'll use; however, having two back up answers is rather rare.

---

12 Zimmerman, A., & Richard, J. (2019, August 16). 5 Unique Interview Questions Every Recruiter Should Ask. Retrieved from https://www.shrm.org/resourcesandtools/hr-topics/employee-relations/pages/five-interview-questions-.aspx

2. Ask them to add two fractions. Yes, two fractions. Try: "What is ½ plus ¾?"

    a. The objective of this question is to see how candidates handle an unexpected question or situation. How does the candidate behave? Did they panic?

3. On a scale of 1 to 10, 10 being the absolute best in the world at your role, where would you rate yourself? And what keeps you from being a 10?

    a. This is a test of both a candidate's ability to select both an area of strength and one of improvement. Additionally, the candidate is required to formulate a plan of action to reach their desired state. This task is very similar to what an employee should be doing during their evaluations with management.

4. Finish this sentence: Most people I
   meet are _________ .

   a. The only answer that should be
      off-limits is 'interesting', as it
      doesn't tell the interviewer
      very much. However, the focus
      of this question is on how
      candidates think about other
      people and what they value in
      those people. If you sense
      judgment or condescension, a
      red flag should go up.

5. Give me the first name of someone
   with whom you work very closely

   a. Hopefully, this answer comes
      rather quickly. More than
      likely, you won't hear their
      supervisor's name. This
      question attempts to illustrate
      how well the candidate builds
      relationships with others at
      work. A quick response with a
      first name and how they met
      should suffice.

- Onboarding Programs: This process is when HR begins to socialize new employees by designing and overseeing the entire onboarding process. During this process, new employees are taught the employer's value system, norms, and desired organizational behaviors. HR needs to ensure that new employees have early job experiences that reinforce the purported culture of the organization. Otherwise, sentiments about new employers can change quickly.

    o For employee orientation programs, experts recommend completing the HR portion of the training in one day. The key components to be reviewed include human resources, safety, key administrative policies, and department overviews.

    o Understand the difference between orientation and onboarding. Orientation lasts a day to a week, while onboarding is a process that lasts up to 12 months. The entire first year of an employee's tenure at a new company should be to introduce them to their job and the jobs that they indirectly 'touch' while working at the organization. Cross-disciplinary training should also occur so that members have an understanding and appreciation for the work of their co-workers. The process includes all evaluations and plans of action as well.

- Reward and Recognition Programs: These programs are key mechanisms that HR can use to motivate employees to engage in behaviors that are in accordance with the culture and values of the organization. Recognition programs, like the employee of the month, are critical for new and existing employees. These programs shine a light on the people that personify the values within the organization.
  - o Companies always look at these as being expensive, but these programs can be both motivating and not costly. For instance, casual Fridays don't cost the business any money. Gift cards or bonus vacation days are inexpensive.

Instead of expensive trainings, try "learning lunches" or lectures that excite people. Corporate charity programs are great. Finally, when all else fails, use food. Food is an excellent motivator for many employees and can be a unique treat for great behavior.

- Performance Management Programs: These would be monthly reviews, 90-day reviews, 6-month reviews, etc. These meetings shouldn't be seen as merely "checking the box" but should be meaningful exchanges in which employees can share their thoughts and feelings in an unbiased environment. Additionally, HR and management should take these opportunities to reinforce the behavioral expectations of the specific employee. All of these meetings should be based on fair and observable behaviors, not speculation.
  - Performance management is an important area that should include performance reviews that are meaningful to both the supervisor and

the employee. The minimum scored
sections (usually 1-5, where 5-
excellent and 1-unacceptable)
included in a performance evaluation
should be:

- Job knowledge
- Quality of work
- Quantity of work
- Reliability
- Initiative and creativity
- Judgment
- Cooperation
- Attendance

(for those with supervisory roles)

- *Planning and organizing*
- *Directing and controlling*
- *Decision-making*
- Noteworthy accomplishments
  during this review period
- Areas requiring improvement
  in job performance (with an
  accompanying performance
  improvement plan)

- Actions taken to improve performance from the previous review.
- Professional development goals
- Overall performance rating
- Employee comments
- Signatures of both parties with the date.

HR is often referred to as the "caretaker" of the organization by many. They are the first group to greet new employees and they are the last group to see most employees. They should always engender the values within the organization and personify those values within all the company's policies and procedures. I took special care to make this section applicable to all businesses and employed examples and explanations that you can use to discuss these ideas with your HR staff.

Bibliography

Anthony, S., & Schwartz, E. (2017, May 8). What the Best Transformational Leaders Do. *Harvard Business Review*. Retrieved from https://hbr.org/2017/05/what-the-best-transformational-leaders-do

Dallas, L. L. (2003). A Preliminary Inquiry into the Responsibility of Corporations and Their Officers and Directors for Corporate Climate: The Psychology of Enron's Demise. *Rutgers LJ, 35*, 1.

Frost, P. J. (2004). Handling Toxic Emotions:: New Challenges for Leaders and their Organization. *Organizational Dynamics, 33*(2), 111-127.

Hofstede, G., Bram, N., Daval, O. D. and Geert, S. (1990) 'Measuring organizational cultures: a qualitative and quantitative study across twenty cases'. Administrative Science Quarterly, 35: 286–316.

Kununu. (2020, January 16). The culture test: 15 great questions to ask about company culture. Retrieved from https://transparency.kununu.com/culture-test-15-great-questions-ask-company-culture/

Northcraft, G. B., Neale, M. A., Tenbrunsel, A., &
Thomas, M. (1996). Benefits and burdens: Does it
really matterWhat we allocate?. *Social Justice
Research*, *9*(1), 27-45.

Permarupan, P. Y., Saufi, R. A., Kasim, R. S. R., &
Balakrishnan, B. K. (2013). The impact of
organizational climate on employee's work passion
and organizational commitment. *Procedia-Social and
Behavioral Sciences*, *107*(2013), 88-95.

Robbins, S. P., & Judge, T. (2019). *Organizational
behavior*. Harlow, England: Pearson Education
Limited.

Schneider, B., Ehrhart, M. G., & Macey, W. H.
(2013). Organizational climate and culture. *Annual
review of psychology*, *64*, 361-388

Veyrat, P. (2017, March 5). 25 Organizational
Climate Survey Questions. Retrieved from
https://www.heflo.com/blog/hr/organizational-
climate-survey-questions/

Warrick, D. D. (2017). What leaders need to know
about organizational culture. *Business
Horizons*, *60*(3), 395-404.

Zimmerman, A., & Richard, J. (2019, August 16). 5 Unique Interview Questions Every Recruiter Should Ask. Retrieved from https://www.shrm.org/resourcesandtools/hr-topics/employee-relations/pages/five-interview-questions-.aspx

Appendix. Leadership Assessment

Key: 1 = Strongly 2 = Disagree 3 = Neutral 4 =
Agree 5 = Strongly disagree agree

1.   I can list my three greatest weaknesses. 1 2 3
4 5

2.   My actions reflect my core values. 1 2 3 4 5

3.   I seek others' opinions before making up my
own mind. 1 2 3 4 5

4.   I openly share my feelings with others. 1 2 3
4 5

5.   I can list my three greatest strengths. 1 2 3 4
5

6.   I do not allow group pressure to control me. 1
2 3 4 5

7.   I listen closely to the ideas of those who
disagree 1 2 3 4 5 with me.

8.   I let others know who I truly am as a person.
1 2 3 4 5

9.   I seek feedback as a way of understanding
who 1 2 3 4 5 I really am as a person.

10.   Other people know where I stand on 1 2 3 4 5 controversial issues.

11.   I do not emphasize my own point of view at the 1 2 3 4 5 expense of others.

12.   I rarely present a "false" front to others. 1 2 3 4 5

13.   I accept the feelings I have about myself. 1 2 3 4 5

14.   My morals guide what I do as a leader. 1 2 3 4 5

15.   I listen very carefully to the ideas of others before 1 2 3 4 5 making decisions.

16.   I admit my mistakes to others. 1 2 3 4 5

1. Sum the responses on items 1, 5, 9, and 13 (self-awareness). 2. Sum the responses on items 2, 6, 10, and 14 (internalized moral perspective). 3. Sum the responses on items 3, 7, 11, and 15 (balanced processing). 4. Sum the responses on items 4, 8, 12, and 16 (relational transparency).

This self-assessment questionnaire is designed to measure your authentic leadership by assessing four components of the process: self-awareness, internalized moral perspective, balanced processing, and relational transparency. By comparing your scores on each of these components, you can determine which are your stronger and which are your weaker components in each category. You can interpret your authentic leadership scores using the following guideline: high = 16–20 and low = 15 and below. Scores in the upper range indicate stronger authentic leadership, whereas scores in the lower range indicate weaker authentic leadership.

Appendix. Toxic Work Environments

This quiz is an excellent evaluation of whether or not toxicity is present in your organization. The quiz combines the elements discussed within the toxic work environments section interactively.

Glassdoor: https://www.glassdoor.com/blog/quiz-is-your-company-toxic/

This quiz by Christine Porath, a published researcher in toxic work environments, was featured in the NY Times and the results compare your organization to those that she has studied in seven different industries: https://www.nytimes.com/interactive/2015/06/21/opinion/sunday/incivility-at-work-quiz.html

This article gives you a list of the top behaviors that you will see in a toxic work environment: https://www.topresume.com/career-advice/how-to-handle-toxic-work-environment

This is a fantastic list of 15 predictive factors of toxic work environments: https://www.predictiveindex.com/blog/15-factors-that-create-a-toxic-workplace/

Appendix. Organizational Climate

What is appreciative inquiry:

https://www.davidcooperrider.com/ai-process/

<u>A Positive Revolution in Change: Appreciative Inquiry</u>:

http://www.tapin.in/Documents/2/Appreciative%20Inquiry%20-%20Positive%20Revolution%20in%20Change.pdf

Appreciative Inquiry: Better Evaluation:

https://www.betterevaluation.org/en/plan/approach/appreciative_inquiry

Appreciative Inquiry: Processes and Applications:

https://positivitystrategist.com/appreciative-inquiry-overview/

Appendix. Organizational Culture

The first thing that I recommend doing is testing your knowledge of organizational culture. SHRM (The Society for Human Resource Management) has a plethora of resources that are backed by actual research:

https://www.shrm.org/resourcesandtools/tools-and-samples/quiz/pages/quiz-what-is-organizational-culture.aspx

Although this quiz uses different terminology, as do many researchers when categorizing types of culture, it is a useful online tool:

https://www.inc.com/articles/2001/08/23312.html

Forbes Magazine Online Culture Quiz:
https://www.forbes.com/sites/lizryan/2016/03/21/take-the-quiz-how-up-to-date-is-your-company-culture/#f29b37031a95

Appendix. Maintaining a Healthy Work Environment

"Creating a more human workplace where employees and business thrive" is the brainchild of SHRM and researchers. This special series was recently published as a special report and contains a slew of amazing insights and recommendations to create and maintain a healthy workplace:

https://www.shrm.org/hr-today/trends-and-forecasting/special-reports-and-expert-views/Documents/Human-Workplace.pdf

The effective workplace index: https://www.shrm.org/hr-today/trends-and-forecasting/special-reports-and-expert-views/Documents/SHRM-NSCW-Effective-Workplace-Index-Brochure.pdf

For those of you with teleworkers, this is a must-read. It is critical to be able to bring teleworkers into the culture of the organization. It isn't always easy, but there are effective ways to do so:

https://www.opm.gov/policy-data-oversight/performance-management/performance-management-cycle/planning/managing-teleworkers-requires-topnotch-performance-management-skills/

https://hbr.org/2012/12/evaluating-the-employees-you-c

https://www.huffpost.com/entry/helping-managers-and-empl_b_4108417

Work-life Balance:

https://www.workflexibility.org/employers-and-employees-must-work-together/